ALL SALAMANCA

Text: M.ª Leticia Sánchez Hernández

Photographer: Manel

Text, photographs, lay-out, design and printing by EDITORIAL ESCUDO DE ORO, S.A.
Rights of total or partial reproduction and translation reserved.
Copyright of this edition for photographs and text: © EDITORIAL ESCUDO DE ORO, S.A.
1st Edition, July 1993 - I.S.B.N. 84-378-1594-0 - Dep. Legal B. 2136-1993

Printed in EEC by FISA - Escudo de Oro, S.A.

Editorial Escudo de Oro, S.A.

An overall view of Salamanca, taken from an old engraving.

INTRODUCTION

Salamanca is considered one of the most important cities in Spain due to its rich historic, artistic and cultural heritage. From prehistoric times right up to the present, this city has witnessed the passing of the most important civilisations which have established themselves on the Iberian Peninsula, whilst civil and religious buildings have been built here as maximum expressions of Spanish and European architecture, and Salamanca has become a cultural centre of the first order thanks to the labour carried out by its two universities.

This book is designed to offer a panoramic view of this exceptional city, offering the visitor the most complete information possible, though limitations of space necessarily make the guide a summary. First, there is a short history of the city, followed by a tour of the monuments of Salamanca. These are grouped into: religious buildings (including cathedrals, churches, monasteries and convents); the universities and colleges; civil buildings (palaces and houses); other notable monuments; squares and gardens; and museums. Finally, the book offers a short section on popular festivities, crafts, gastronomy and bullfighting.

HISTORY OF THE CITY

The history of Salamanca goes back to the times of the prehistoric settlements on the banks of the River Tormes. Later, legend has it that the area was inhabited by three important civilisations, one after the other: the Ligurians, the Celts and the Iberians. There is a Celtic site, a Verraco settlement, of which there are many on the Meseta, in the proximity of the Roman bridge. This bridge has been a symbol of the city since time immemorial, and now forms part of the coat of arms of Salamanca. It was, however, during the occupation of the last of these tribes, the Iberians, in the 3rd century BC, that Salamanca truly came into existence as a growing centre of population, fast becoming a city. Over the following centuries, this tendency was converted into a reality. As a reminder of Iberian times, and in a fair state of conservation, is the so-called Gate of Hannibal, commemorating the wars between the Romans and the Carthaginians.

Of all the civilisations which have reigned over Salamanca, the Roman period is the most notable. The Romans included the city in the province of Lusitania and embellished it with monuments, some of which can still be admired, such as the bridge, part of the city walls and the famous Via (or Path) de la Plata.

Under the Visigoths, the city became known as Salmantica, and it was during the reign of Recaredo that coins began to be minted here. The reign of Leovigildo saw the arrival of a number of nobles here, come to force the rebellious inhabitants of Salamanca to submit to the new ruler.

The Moorish invasion engendered a Saracen enclave here, later conquered by Alfonso I of León during the war waged to liberate the cities to the south of the River Duero. Whilst in Christian hands, the Moors laid siege to Salamanca several times in an attempt to regain their lost dominions. Firstly, by Abderrhaman in the year 903, repelled by Ramiro, and later, by Almanzor, who took the city, wreaking havoc on its

The University seal, carved in the keystone of the vault.

Coat of Arms of Salamanca City Council.

The best way to enter Salamanca is on foot, over the Roman bridge, where we will see the cathedrals awaiting us.

inhabitants until Alfonso VI finally completed the definitive conquest in 1102, entrusting Raymond of Burgundy with its repopulation.

The ties binding the city of Salamanca with its episcopal See, founded in the year 589, have always been very strong, though during the Moorish occupations its prelates were forced to take refuge in Oviedo. Alfonso VI restored the See in 1102, at the same time as the repopulation of the city began, and on the same Visigoth site where building was beginning on the Romanesque Cathedral of Santa María.

A decree for the repopulation of Salamanca being published, the city was occupied by various groups, who settled in clearly-differentiated districts: the Castilians occupied the north, the highlanders and mountain dwellers the west, the Portuguese and Galicians the central quarters, the Mozarabs and Jews the south. Due to this huge diversity of settlers, Salamanca became composed of seven districts or colaciones, ruled over by a local government made up of a mayor and a jury and by the parishes of each quarter. Ethnic violence was also sparked off, with grave disturbances which caused, among other unfortunate events, the defeat of the city at the hands of the Moors in 1137. This military disaster forced Count Ponce of Cabrera to take the inhabitants to task and to order them to submit as one to his authority in order to prevent future debacles.

During the Middle Ages, Salamanca gradually grew up into a religious and university centre of great

The cathedrals are reflected in all their beauty in the waters of the Tormes.

importance. The cathedrals were built and the university founded, accompanied by a large number of monasteries and convents and university colleges, whilst the fame of the city spread, attracting the visit of innumerable famous personages. Among the most outstanding events during this period were the baptism of Alfonso XI in the cathedral, the location in the city of the headquarters of the troops of John II of Portugal in 1410, and the preaching and teaching of some of the most famous religious leaders and professors of the times. Nevertheless, the city was not immune to the vagaries of the turbulent 14th century, and witnessed many a bloody struggle between rival families in open warfare, as well as the tragic confrontation between the followers of Santo Tomé and Saint Benito in El Corrillo de la Hierba. In 1467, Henry IV, to reward the services of the people of Salamanca, awarded the city the right to hold a fair during the first week of September. In 1497, the Catholic Monarchs also granted the rival bands of Saint Benito and Saint Tomé a number of concessions and privileges. Queen Isabel also honoured the city with her many visits.

During the 16th century, Salamanca was the first city whose parliamentarians refused Charles V the levy he had requested in 1516 in order to bring the situation in the Low Countries under control. This defiant act cost those responsible exile and the loss of their votes in the parliament. Salamanca also played an active part in the War of the Communities of Castile, contributing 6,000 troops.

Dusk in Salamanca, the cathedral towers rising stately over the city.

Due to its character as a university city, Salamanca is associated with the the group of most important such cities in Spain: Seville, Valladolid, Granada, Toledo, Santiago, Medina del Campo and, in more modern times, Madrid and Alcalá. Such eminence has made the city the object of numerous visits on the part of the rulers of the houses of Austria and Bourbon. The visits of the Catholic Queen, Isabel, were followed by those of the Emperor Charles V in 1534; that of his son, Philip II, who marred María of Portugal here in 1543; the visit of Philip III and Margaret of Austria in 1600 (as we shall see later, these monarchs founded important religious sites here); and, in the 18th century, the visit of Philip V, after the War of Succession.

It was, in fact, after the advent of the Bourbon dynasty in 1700 that Salamanca aligned itself unconditionally on the side of the king of France against the pretensions of the Austrian archduke.

As a last important event in the history of the city, we can speak of the role played by Salamanca in the War of Independence when, in 1809, it was invaded by the French. After some years of domination and the looting a important buildings, the French were defeated by the Duke of Wellington at the Battle of Salamanca, or of Arapiles, on 22 July 1812. Besides these outstanding historical events, of course, Salamanca has played a part in the development of Spain from its foundation until modern times.

The monument to Miguel de Unamuno. ▷

The monument to Lazarillo de Tormes. ▽

AN OVERALL VIEW OF SALAMANCA AND ITS PEOPLE

Salamanca can well be defined as an architectural museum. The entire city is replete with admirable sites, in which every corner, every square, every street, every church or palace, everything, contains fine fronts, splendid coats of arms or lovely wrought-iron work, which transport the visitor back to the legends and historic episodes enacted here in the past. Not for nothing have so many writers and poets situated the action of their novels and verses in Salamanca. Some examples are «El Lazarillo de Tormes», the poems of Friar Luis de León, «The Student of Salamanca», by Espronceda, the journey described by Antonio Ponz, the impressions narrated by Miguel de Unamuno, the chronicles of such illustrious historians as González Dávila, Dorado, Falcón and Villar Macias, and so on. Turning to 20th-century writers, we cannot overlook Tormo, Gómez Moreno, Camón Aznar, Sánchez Cantón, Rodríguez G. de Ceballos, Chueca Goitia and Gaya Nuño, among whom are some of the most important authors to have chosen Salamanca as their subject matter.

Salamanca is known as a scholarly, university and courtly city. All its monuments help to build up a picture of its historic and cultural importance and character. Its two cathedrals, the old and the new, of which few cities can boast, are an expression of Romanesque, Gothic, Renaissance and Baroque art. The Monastery of San Esteban and the front of the university are examples of the purest Spanish Plateresque architecture. The innumerable courtyards of the city, such as those of Escuelas or the Colegio Fonseca, and cloisters such as those of Las Dueñas or the former College of the Society of Jesus, now the Pontifical University, and many more jewels contained in this treasure chest of a city, feature mostly Renaissance and Baroque nooks hidden from sight, adorning the arches, columns and splendid sculpted capitals. And what can we say of the magnificent altarpieces of the churches of La Purísima, el Santo

(Next page 8-9): Aerial photo of the cathedrals.

◁ *Vieira shells and fleurs-de-lis, engraved into the stone.*

▽ *The fine Gothic grilles of the Casa de las Conchas.*

Espíritu, Las Ursulas or La Vera Cruz, Churrigueresque to the core all, as well as milestones in the history of Spanish art? We could also mention such characteristic monuments as the Casa de las Conchas, the Palace of Monterrey, Plaza Mayor (without a doubt one of the most beautiful squares in the whole of Spain, and the nerve centre of Salamanca), the towers of El Clavero and La Clerecía, of great interest not only because of their singular beauty, but also because, rising over this monumental city, they command magnificent, unique, overall views of Salamanca. These famous towers, a list of which would not be complete without mention of the breathtaking Torre del Gallo in the Old Cathedral, standing out against the sky, possess unrivalled loveliness seen from the Roman bridge at dusk, when the city is enveloped in a haze reflecting the Tormes, the colour of the sky and the hues of the golden stones of Salamanca.

The remarkable colour of this stone, the gilded, soft stone from the quarries of Villamayor, is a constant feature in all the monuments of Salamanca, allowing façades, capitals, windows and all other elements capable of bearing adornment to be embellished with reliefs and details reminiscent of the work of silversmiths, and for this reason the style has been baptised with the name of «Plateresque», the single style which distinguishes the city of Salamanca. However, the enormous artistic importance of the city is not derived solely from the architecture of its civil and religious buildings, but also from the artistic treasures contained within the walls of these. For example, the chapels of the cathedrals, the magnificent altarpiece by Nicolás Florentino in the Old Cathedral, the famous triptych by John of Flanders in the City Museum, or the «Inmaculada», by Ribera, presiding the high altar of the Church of the Purísima in the Convent of Recollet Augustines.

As the visitor tours the many monuments in Salamanca, contemplating the fronts of palaces and

A lovely close-up of the Gothic grille over one of the windows of the Casa de las Conchas.

churches and entering one building after another to admire the works of art contained in them, he or she will also perceive a singular quality in the city and its inhabitants, a feature remarked on by all the travellers who have passed through it and by all the writers who have attempted to describe the spirit of the place. The heart of Salamanca is to be found in and around Plaza Mayor, where natives and visitors alike congregate to chat, to relax at the pavement cafés under the arches, to shop at the establishments in the square itself or in the surrounding streets, or simply to contemplate its architectural forms, especially those of the City Hall. The bustle of the square formerly reached its height, and still does, though to a lesser extent, with the traditional strolls under the arcades of groups of young men going clockwise, and of young men going in the opposite direction, so that, from time to time, the desired meetings would take place. To this tradition has been added, over the years, summer concerts held in the square, which attract hundreds of young people, the night life in the fashionable bars and cafés, and the meetings of livestock farmers who come from all over the province to gather here. Plaza Mayor is a typically Mediterranean forum, in which life takes place out of doors, in the street, the café, around the shops and monuments: a place where culture and day-to-day life reach their maximum expression.

Another aspect of the life of Salamanca is formed by the trappings of its university, concentrated in the old University district, but which impregnates the entire city. The many students who come here from other Spanish cities or from foreign countries give the city a youthful, animated spirit, combined with scholarly curiosity and a desire to welcome all those seeking education here. Salamanca is, then, a hospitable, many-faceted city in which there is a place for everyone. Moreover, its traditional teachings, principally centred on the humanities, besides making its university one of the most prestigious in the world, have

A view of Plaza Mayor.

also imbued the city with an awareness of its mission of transmitting the most profound, deeply-rooted cultural values.

The university, religious and cattle-farming nature of Salamanca, fruit of the three main elements of the city, its university, its religious institutions and its bull-fighting, have formed the basis of its character and atmosphere. Regarding the character of the people, it has always said that Castilians, and the people of Salamanca in particular, have a rather strict, sober quality. It is certainly true that the natives of Castile, perhaps due to the climate and countryside, harsh and dry, to which these people have had to adapt since times immemorial, appear austere and short-spoken. However, they are also sincere, generous and keen for the visitor to feel at home here. There is no doubt that the inhabitants of Salamanca make an exceptional contribution to making it a cosmopolitan, open city, giving a warm welcome to all who choose to stop here.

A charming night-time view of Plaza Mayor with, in the background, the City Hall.

The Enrique Esteban bridge and the cathedrals.

Plaza Mayor is the most splendid meeting-point in the city.

A view of the City Hall from the Pabellón de San Ma...

Plaza Mayor at dusk.

LOCATION AND CLIMATE

Salamanca lies in the southwest of the Community of Castilla y León, on the foothills of the Central Mountain System, on a hard, almost completely flat granite peneplain. Average height above sea level is 830 metres, high ground, then, though lower than the lands of Avila. Running through the city is the River Tormes, which has its source in the Sierra de Gredos and its mouth on the Atlantic coast of Portugal.

The height of the city determines its climate, characterised by sharp drops in temperature in winter and low rainfall throughout the year. In summer, due to tropical air masses, the climate is dry. Average temperatures are 3°C in winter and 22°C in summer, when temperatures of up to 40°C are reached.

Plaza Mayor opens before us from the Pabellón de Petrineros, opposite the Pabellón Real, in whose centre is the Arch of San Fernando.

The central apse and dome of the Old Cathedral.

◁ *An impressive view of Plaza Mayor at dusk (p.16-17).*

RELIGIOUS BUILDINGS

THE CATHEDRALS

Old Cathedral

The Romanesque Cathedral of Santa María was built on the same site as the Visigoth See at the end of the 12th century, as part of the work of repopulating the city after the Christian reconquest. The first document referring to its construction dates back to 1149, the last to 1289, from which it can be deduced that the

Pedro Petriz left us this beautiful tower, with its double row of windows under a scaled dome, crowned by a weather vane whose cock («gallo») gives its name to the tower.

Slender, robust pillars forming an elegant procession along the nave.

work took one and a half centuries. The building was built in various stages, the first including the and foot, with the oldest elements, the porch and the apse and aisles. In the second stage, the side chapels were completed with pointed vaults and the transept vaulted. Finally, the roof of the transept was completed with the addition of the dome known as the Torre del Gallo, and the nave and aisles roofed. It appears that various hands were responsible for the roofs: one person carried out those of the Torre del Gallo and the aisles nearby, as well as the first two stretches of the nave, whilst another person directed work on the roofs of the ends of the transept and the first stretches of the aisles, whilst, lastly, a third person was responsible for the final stretches of the nave.

To bear the weight of the new system of vaults, corbels were adjoined to the springs of the arches of these vaults, disguised by sculptures of devils and fantastic animals. The capitals are varied, with no particular overall pattern: there are floral motifs, curved leaves, palms, acanthus and biblical scenes.

The outstanding features of the nave and aisles are: the Chapel of San Martín, a magnificent example of Gothic painting, with an altarpiece in a natural niche, with figures representing angels, prophets and saints al tempera, with a wealth of colours. Next to this on one side is the tomb of Bishop Rodrígo Díaz, and on the other are more tombs of a similar construction, with embedded altars.

The high chapel contains one of the most beautiful 15th-century Spanish altarpieces, and one of the most important works of art in Spain. It consists of 53 panels depicting the life of Christ and the Virgin Mary, divided into five storeys with eleven columns. The contract for this was signed by Nicolás Florentino, and though his hand can be noted in the work, there is no doubt that other painters were involved. The panels are in a wholly universal Gothic style, characterised by elongated figures, calligraphic lines and a profusion of

The Old Cathedral: side aisle featuring mensule with a fantastic animal.

In the transept are the extraordinary tombs of Arch-deacon Diego Garci-López (1342), bearing a sculpture of the procession of the Magi; that of a benefactress of the cathedral, Doña Elena (1272), imitating the system of the Torre del Gallo; that of Precentor Aparicio Guillén (1287); and that of Alfonso Vidal, Dean of Avila, a late-13th-century work.

The cloister, restored after the Lisbon earthquake in 1755, was constructed at the same time as the cathedral itself. It is reached through a door of wreathed columns, with capitals and perforated oculi. The most outstanding element of the cloister is the western corner, which conserves late-12th-century arches and capitals. The southern gallery has a lovely altar-piece of the Virgen de la Estrella, dating back to the mid-16th century and painted in the style of John of Flanders, and the tomb of Archdeacon Gutiérrez de Castro, by John of Juni.

The galleries of the cloister open into several chapels. Beginning with the east gallery, we start with the Chapel of Talavera, with groined stellar vaults, ribbed with different mouldings in small columns inserted between the windows of the tambour. The ribs intertwine to form eight-pointed stars. The altarpiece and sculptures are attributed to the Italian Lucas Mitata, and the panels to the school of Berruguete. The chapel is enclosed by a magnificent Plateresque iron grille, forged in Toledo.

Next is the Chapel of Sant Bárbara, founded in 1334 by Bishop Juan Lucero. In the centre are the tombs of the founder, García Ruíz (1359), and Bertrán Bertránez, dating back to the same period. Round the walls are rough stones where university professors and doctors would sit to examine students, who sat on the monk's chair now placed behind the tomb of García Ruíz. If the candidate passed the test successfully, he would leave in triumph through the cathedral; if not, he would have to take his exit through the Puerta de Carros.

Turning now to the west gallery, we come to the Chapel of Santa Catalina, founded in 1392 and later extended to house the library of Bishop Gonzalo Vivero. The chapel has a fine roof, with tierceron

colour and architectural background. Over the altar-piece is the statue of the patron saint of Salamanca, the Virgen de la Vega, which was originally in the Augustine monastery which stood on the banks of the Tormes. The carving dates back to the 12th century and is decorated with Limoges enamel. Also outstanding in this same high chapel are the tombs of the archdeacons Fernando Alonso (1279) and Diego Arias (1360), as well as those of bishops Gonzalo Vivero (1480) and Sancho de Castilla (1446).

The altarpiece of the Old Cathedral: 53 splendid sections illustrating the lives of Christ and the Virgin. In the vault, a superb fresco depicting the Final Judgement.

Capital of the nave: Samson hamstringing a lion, in the presence of masks and monsters.

vaults, and a portrait of Gregorio Fernández de Liébana, president of the Chancellory of Valladolid, attributed to Sánchez Coello.

Our tour of the cloister ends at the Chapel of Los Anaya or of San Bartolomé, founded in 1422 by Diego de Anaya y Maldonado, archbishop of Seville and founder of the famous University College of San Bartolomé. The roof has tierceron vaults, with a stellar front. In one corner is an organ with Mudéjar woodwork and tribune. The outstanding feature of this chapel is the tomb of its founder, by an anonymous artist known as the «Master of Los Anaya», possibly a Spanish sculptor familiar with the style and techniques of Burgundy. These he united with elements of international Gothic art. The tomb is in alabaster,

and is surrounded by a wrought-iron grille dated at around 1514. To the sides are the tombs of relatives of Don Diego, with remarkable Renaissance elements.

The Old Cathedral of Salamanca is an outstanding Spanish Romanesque monument, forming part of the Castilian-Leones tradition, in turn strongly linked to the Road to Santiago, like the cathedrals of Santiago de Compostela, Toro and Zamora. These are all, generally speaking, constructions with a dome resting on a transept, perfectly visible from the exterior, with smaller towers acting as buttresses. The Church of the Monastery of Santo Domingo in Silos, now destroyed, must also have been in this style.

Chapel of San Martín, or del Aceite (Old Cathedral): Tomb of Bishop Rodrigo Díaz.

*A view of
the nave of
the Old
Cathedral.*

New Cathedral: the vault covering the High Chapel, a lovely composition of groins and keystones.

New Cathedral

The fact that the city of Salamanca possesses two cathedrals is a rather singular circumstance which came about due to the decision to build a new place of worship to accommodate the large number of students attending the university. The New Cathedral was designed to stand tangent to the Old Cathedral, on the highest hill, commanding splendid views. The foundation stone was laid in 1512, and Juan Gil de Hontañón was designated master builder, succeeded on his death by his son, Juan Gil the Younger, and subsequently by Juan de Ibarra and Juan de Alava. In 1538, Rodrígo Gil de Hontañón took charge. The cathedral was constructed in various stages, the first dating from 1512-13 to 1560, the second from 1589 until the early 17th century, and the third from 1668 to 1733. In all, it took 200 years to complete the cathedral.

The exterior is characterised by a system of buttresses and flying buttresses topped by the sharply-pointed spires, balanced by the horizontal planes of the crenellations and balustrades. The naves are of staggered height, with soaring dome and main front. This main front was designed by Juan Gil de Hontañón and is composed of five sections separated by buttresses and protected by arches and ornate vaults, especially the ogee arches of the door, with various

A splendid view of the columns, vault and dome of the New Cathedral.

series of arches. The bays are decorated with baldachins, statues, heraldic motifs and medallions. Various sculptors worked on this masterpiece: John of Gante, for example, is thought to have carved the Calvary over the entrance, whilst the Birth of Christ and the Apostles flanking it, as well as the Immaculate in the mullions, completed in 1661, are the work of an unknown artist from Valladolid.

The interior closely resembles the arrangement of Seville Cathedral. It is in the form of a Latin cross divided into five sections of different heights, crossed by simple aisles. The pillars consist of slender columns scarcely broken by atrophied capitals from which the vault ribs spring, according to the nave, a varied combination of tiercions. Over the transept is the imposing cathedral dome.

The high chapel is now covered by crimson velvet, over which is the fine «Assumption of the Virgin», the patron saint of the cathedral, by Esteban de Rueda. The ostensory and altar are made of marble, and were brought from the Church of San Sebastián. On either side are silver urns containing the relics of Saint John of Sahagún and Saint Thomas of Villanueva.

Side door to the New Cathedral, reached by the Patio Chico.

New Cathedral: the choir, organ and spring of the vault.

the most important chapels in the cathedral and one
of the finest monuments in Salamanca. Richly
ornamented in a style similar to the main front, this
chapel has a splendid 16th-century ceramic socle and
a magnificent altarpiece, sculpted by John of Gante.
The third chapel was founded by the president of the
Chancellory of Valladolid, Gregorio Fernández de
Liébana, in 1577. Its importance resides in the paintings in the altarpiece, the upper canvas representing
the Apparition of Christ Resuscitated to the Virgin», a
copy of one of Navarre's compositions for the cloisters of the Monastery of El Escorial. The lower painting depicts «The Burial of Christ» and is another copy,
this time of a work by Titian, in the Prado. The fourth
chapel, formerly the passage to the transept of the
Old Cathedral, is presided over by an altarpiece created by Antonio García Ramiro in 1627. This side of
the building is completed by the chapel containing the
Altarpiece of the Virgen del Desagravio (thus known
because atonement was made in its honour after it
was profaned in 1664). This was the first altarpiece in
Salamanca to incorporate wreathed columns.
Next are the chapels of the ambulatory. The first of
these is the Chapel of El Nazareno, also known as the
Chapel of San Roque, containing a gilt altarpiece on a
blue background, part of a number commissioned to
complete the altarpieces in the chapels of the ambu-
latory. This contains copies of two works by Andrea
Sacchi. Opposite the altarpiece is the statue of «San
Francisco de Paula», by Bernardo Pérez de Robles.
The Chapel of San Nicolás de Bari contains a sculpture
of the saint, by José de Larra. Next is the outstanding
Chapel of San José, with an altarpiece by Alejandro
Carnicero, and providing access to the sculpture «La
Piedad», by Luis Salvador Carmona (1760). The chapel
in the trasaltar exhibits the crucifix said to have been
carried by The Cid, a Byzantine carving of Christ in
Majesty dating back to the late-11th century. It is kept
in the altarpiece, which is by Alberto de Churriguera.

The choir and trascoro are by Alberto de Churriguera
between 1732 and 1738. The choirstalls are one of
the finest examples of Spanish Baroque art, and are
by Joaquín de Churriguera, his brothers and Alejandro
Carnicero. The organ on the left is by Damián Luis
(1568) and the one on the right was a gift from Bishop
José Sancho Granado, made by the royal organist
Pedro de Echevarría in 1745. The area is enclosed by
a Rococo grille by Joseph Duperier.
All the chapels in the cathedral, both those of the
aisles and those of the ambulatory, have an identical
structure: altar located on the east side, and on the
other walls niches under ogee arches flanked by
spires. Beginning with the south aisle, the first chapel,
dedicated to Saint Lawrence, was founded in 1630 by
the then mayor of the city, Sánchez Aceves. This
chapel contains an altarpiece in the style of Francisco
de la Oya. Next is the «Golden Chapel», or Chapel of
Todos los Santos, founded in 1525 by the Archdeacon
of Alba, Francisco Sánchez Palanzuela. This is one of

New Cathedral: Chapel of El Santísimo: the beautiful Pietà sculpted by Salvador Carmona in around 1760, one of the last Castilian Baroque images.

The next chapel contains an altarpiece by Joaquín de Churriguera, with a «Virgen de la Soledad», by Benlliure. The Chapel of El Pilar is presided over by a 14th-statue of the saint, with the singular feature that it depicts the Child playing the lute. The chapels of the ambulatory are completed by that of San Tirso.

The chapels of the north aisle were the first to be constructed and are the work of Juan Gil de Hontañón. The first is the Chapel of San Antonio, containing an 18th-century altarpiece. The next was founded in 1628 by Antonio Corrionero, Bishop of the Canaries and of Salamanca, and was conceived as the pantheon of its founder and his family. The chapel contains the outstanding tombs of the bishop himself (1633), of his brother (1594) and of Antonio Ribera Corrionero (1660). The following chapel is the one founded by Canon Antonio de Almansa y Vera, with an altarpiece dedicated to Saint James and Saint Theresa (1628). Finally, we come to the Chapel of San Clemente, with an 18th-century altarpiece containing two paintings, one of them by Carlos Maratta (1661). The sacristy consists of two dependencies, the antesacristía, or prebendaries' room, constructed in 1731 by Manuel de Larra Churriguera, and the sacristía mayor, built in 1755 by Juan de Sagarvinaga. Finally, there is the interesting custodia del Corpus, a monstrance contained in the reliquary, with a splendid 15th-century capitel, tabernacle and Plateresque plinth (1547), with bier designed by Alberto de Churriguera in 1728.

The New Cathedral of Salamanca pertains to those built during the final phase of the Gothic cathedrals of Castilia-León, and, like Seville and Granada cathedrals, was completed at the end of the 14th century. Flemish and German artists contributed their skills to the glory of these cathedrals, which are characterised by their flamboyant Gothic style. These are buildings of profuse decoration, designed to dazzle the faithful and to proclaim the splendour and power of cities enjoying a period of commercial and cultural greatness.

An overall view of the Church of San Marcos.

An overall view of the Church of Sancti Spiritus.

CHURCHES

Church of San Martín
(Plaza del Corrillo)

This lovely Romanesque church was founded in 1103 by Martín Fernández, leader of the colonists who came from Toro to repopulate the city. The original building was completed between the second half of the 12th century and the beginning of the next, but the damage suffered during the 18th century and the destruction of the altarpiece in a fire in 1854 obliged a complete restoration of the church. Strongly influenced by the architecture of Toro, Saint Martin's consists of a nave and two aisles without transept, separated by columns whose capital are adorned variously with accanthus leaves, plain leaves and allegorical figures. The aisles are covered by groined vaults, the nave by an acute cannon vault. The sanctuary contains three chapels with apses. At the foot of the nave, the height of the vault allowed the construction of a gallery, with a choir at the front. The main altarpiece, by Alberto de Churriguera (1731)

was brought here from the Church of San Sebastián to replace the altarpiece destroyed by fire in 1854. The church also contains the tombs of Pedro de Paz, Pedro de Santisteban and his wife, Isabel Nieta, and Luis Yáñez, all in Flemish Gothic style. The south front features two pairs of Corinthian columns whose entablature contains a niche flanked by columns and frontispiece in the same style, enclosing a sculpture of Saint Martin. The north front is a beautiful Romanesque gate with semicircular archivolts, veritable jewels of Salamancan Romanesque art.

Church of San Marcos
(Plaza de San Marcos)

Founded in around 1178, this was the parish church of the district occupied by settlers from Castile. Building began in 1202. The church has the peculiarity of a circular groundplan, interrupted by three semicircular apses. The area is divided into six sections separated by groined arches spreading out from the columns. The ceiling is Moorish, with a framework of rafters in a complex, interwoven design. The exterior features a relief of Saint Mark, seated and writing.

Mudéjar coffering in the choir of the Church of Sancti Spiritus.

Church of Sancti Spiritus
(Cuesta del Sancti Spiritus)

Founded in around 1190 in the Toro district, in 1223 this church was given to the Order of Saint James by Alfonso IX. In 1268, the Grand Master of the Order donated it to the Convent of Las Dueñas which, after a series of vicissitudes, was dissolved by Charles III in 1786. The building (built 1530-1540) owes much to the style of Juan Gil, and its interior is very similar to that of the Monastery of San Esteban.

The choir is an outstanding feature of this church, and features a magnificent tiled floor and Gothic stalls, but what has really contributed to its fame is the Moorish coffered ceiling, with coffered panels decorated with stars, honeycombs and rosettes, with a side gallery and a honeycomb cornice. The ceiling is covered with gold and chiaroscuro paintings of grotesque themes on a blue background.

The main altarpiece, dating back to 1659, is by the school of Gregorio Fernández. To the sides of the presbytery are the tombs of the founders, Martín Alfonso and María Meléndez, made in around the year 1270. The exterior features buttresses adorned with two orders of pinnacles.

Church of Santa María de la Vega

This church dates back to the year 1150 and was consecrated to the patron saint of Salamanca. From 1166 until the reign of Ferdinand II, it was under the domination of the Monastery of San Isidoro de León and its abbot. The church was completely rebuilt in the 14th century and consists of a nave and two

◁ *The splendid altar in the Church of Sancti Spiritus.*

A Romanesque statue of Christ in the Church of Sancti Spiritus.
▽

Statue of the Virgen de la Vega. ▽

Romanesque apses in the Church of Santo Tomás Cantuariense, or of Canterbury.

aisles, with a high chapel and camarín dating back to 1718. At the foot of the church is a choir, covered by a vault featuring adorned coffering between its arches. The south nave features a stone relief depicting Christ dead in the arms of His mother, recalling the altarpiece of the Church of Fuenteguinaldo and some of the works of Rodrigo Gil. Of the original building, some Romanesque arches forming the cloister remain. These are reminiscent of the churches of Silos, Aguilar de Campoo and Santa María de Nieva.

Church of San Cristóbal
(Plaza de San Cristóbal)

Founded in 1145 by the Knights Hospitallers, this church is in the form of a Latin cross with one apse and side chapels. The high chapel has a barrel vault resting on two pillars. The capitals are similar to those in San Isidoro in León, and to a number of churches in Avila.

Church of Santo Tomás de Cantuariense
(Paseo de Canalejas)

Also known as Santo Tomás de Canturianense, this church was built by the Portuguese in 1175. It has the form of a Latin cross, and its apses contain three chapels. There is a stone retable with Ionic pillars and an Italian panel representing the Virgin offering the Child a basket of fruit. Though completely restored, some of the original Romanesque elements can still be observed. The exterior is in stone with decorative small arches in the buttresses.

Church of San Juan de Barbalos
(Calle del Horno)

Founded in 1232 by the Knights Hospitallers, this church has a single nave, in the style of the cathedral and churches of Zamora, with semi-circular apse and high chapel with barrel vault. At the foot of the church are the remains of a tower, and the door is on the north side, enclosed in semicircular arches. The cloister was restored in the 16th century. The building contains the fine Cristo de la Zarza, a walnut wood crucifix, and an altarpiece with two al tempera paintings on canvas, dating back to the 14th century and depicting the Baptism of Christ, and Herod and Herodias.

Church of San Julián
(Calle del Obispo Jarrín)

Also known as the Church of San Julián and Santa Basilsa, it was founded in 1107 by the settlers from Toro. Of its original Romanesque structure, all that remains is the south wall, with a decoratively sculptured porch, and the towers at the foot of the church.

Front of the Church of San Polo.

An impressive view of the sanctuary of the Romanesque Mudéjar Church of Santiago.

Inside is a Baroque altarpiece by Alonso de Balbás, and a painting of «La Inmaculada» by José Antolínez (1662). Another fine work in this church is the alabaster sculpture representing «The Virgen de los Remedios», dating back to the late-15th century.

Church of San Polo
(Calle de San Pablo)

The Church of San Polo, or of San Pablo, was founded in 1108 in the Portuguese quarter. The building is a mixture of Romanesque and Moorish elements, and was restored during the 16th century. There is a nave and two aisles, with three chapels. The walls are decorated inside and out with decorative series of arches.

Church of Santiago
(Plaza del Puente)

Founded in 1145, this is the only Mozarab church remaining in the city. The three apses, plastered outside and and in ashlar throughout, retain their original cornices with double moulding. In the central apse, decorative series of arches can be admired. The interior of the church has been restored.

Church of Santa María de los Caballeros
(Calle de Bordadores)

Now known as the Church of Las Adoratrices, as it was used by nuns of this order. It was founded as a parish church in 1194, though it was rebuilt in 1581. It consists of a nave and two aisles with four semicircular arches on columns with Corinthian capitals. The high chapel is covered by a Mudéjar ceiling. The 16th-century altarpiece contains three sections, the first Ionic, the second Corinthian and the last featuring two wreathed columns with Baroque sculptures in the style of Becerra, and a number of panels. However, the most important work here is the alabaster tomb of Alfonso Rodríguez Guedejas, by the author of that of Bishop Anaya in the Old Cathedral.

Convent of La Anunciación.

Calle de Bordadores.

Church of the Vera Cruz
(Calle de Sorias)

Originally built in the second half of the 16th century, this church was reformed in 1714. Of the original construction, only a porch with a statue of the Virgen remains. The interior is Baroque in style, after Churriguera. It contains the following works of interest: «La Inmaculada», by Gregorio Fernández; «La Soledad», by Felipe del Corral; and a number of *pasos* (floats) used during the Holy Week processions, by Alejandro Carnicero.

◁ Altar of the Church of La Vera Cruz.

Magnificent sculptures adorning the front of the Church of San Esteban.

CONVENTS AND MONASTERIES

Monastery of San Esteban
(Plaza de San Esteban)

The Monastery of San Esteban was begun in 1525 by order of Friar Juan Alvarez de Toledo, Bishop of Cordova, according to plans drawn up by John of Alava, and was completed in 1618. The site contains a church, the Cloister de Reyes, sacristy, chapterhouse, Cloister de profundis, gatehouse, library and Cloister of los Aljibes.

The church is in the form of a Latin cross, with a single nave covered by ogees up to the crossing, which is in Renaissance style, both in the balustrade and in the striated mouldings crowned by Corinthian capitals on which it rests. Above is a lantern with twelve windows, each divided by a Baroque cross and culminating in a semi-circular arch. The choir is situated over a segmental vault and contains seats carved in ashlar by Alfonso Balbás (1651-1658). Over the prior's seat is a splendid Baroque carving of Saint Dominic, and a painting of «La Virgen», of the school of Rubens. In the centre is the lectern, with 16th- and 17th-century choirbooks. The lunula is decorated with an interpretation of Rubens' «The Triumph of the Church», by Palomino. The high altarpiece was constructed from 1692-1693 by José de Churriguera. It consists of wreathed columns covered by vines, leaves and grapes. Over the enormous Corinthian columns is a simply-decorated entablature over which is a large semi-circular arch with a painting of Claudio Coello depicting «The Martyrdom of Saint Stephen». This, in turn, is flanked by a profusion of Baroque carvings. On either side of the altar are niches containing statues of Saint Dominic and Saint Francis. Right of the crossing is the altar of Saint Dominic, with a statue of the saint attributed to Salvador Carmona, whilst to the right is that of Saint Thomas, with paintings by Pitti. The side chapels contains 16th- and 17th-century carvings.

The main front was constructed around 1660, and consists of a series of arches decorated in the interior and flanked by buttresses. The door opens under an arch formed by fine beading in the jambs, with three pillars on either side, between which are statues of saints of the Order. Above is a frieze with medallions and coats of arms and, higher up, nine pillars and dossels forming the tympanum, adorned with a «Martyrdom of Saint Stephen». This is the work of Juan Antonio Ceroni (1610), and the artist's name appears here, carved in the stone. Over these pillars is another frieze, leading to the altarpiece, which corresponds to the arcade depicting a Calvary crowned by an Italianate Eternal Father. The last section is formed by a terrace with balustrade, flanked by small turrets with perforated spires.

Choir of the Church and Convent of San Esteban.

«The Triumph of the Church», a final mural by Antonio Palomino, which decorates the back of the choir of the Church of San Esteban.

The altarpiece in the high altar in the Church of San Esteban.

The impressive volumes of the Church of San Esteban and the Convent of Los P.P. Dominicos seen from Plaza del Concilio de Trento.

The Claustro de Reyes, reached from the left wing of the crossing, is in Plateresque Gothic style, particularly marked in the lower section, which contains twenty large windows divided by three mullions and a Gothic vault. The exterior has flying buttresses decorated with slender columns reaching up to the upper gallery and crowned by a cornice with 40 arches supported by square pillars. The upper gallery is covered by a wooden square-tiled roof.

The Soto staircase, situated in the vestibule of the sacristy, is a hanging staircase in predominantly Plateresque style dating back to 1553. It is composed of thick, rounded pillars with striations, with a classical balustrade. The last section features a polychrome stone relief of Mary Magdalene.

The sacristy is a large room, and was founded by Friar Pedro de Herrera, Bishop of Tuy. It consists of thick pillars between frontons, topped by Corinthian capi-

The fine lines of the cloister vaults convert this site into a veritable petrified palm forest.

tals and crowned by a Renaissance cornice supporting arches on which rests a vault with lunettes adorned with bosses. The rich liturgical ornaments of the monastery are kept in huge walnut chests.

The chapterhouse, reached through the Puerta de San Esteban in the cloister, is in a sombre Baroque style. It is formed by pillars crowned by Doric capitals with a wide cornice. Inside is a Corinthian altar.

The De profundis cloister adjoins the chapterhouse, and is situated on the other side of the Puerta de San Gregorio y Santo Tomás de Aquino. It was completed in 1550 by order of the Catholic Monarchs, and

Cloister of Los Reyes de San Esteban.

The sacristy of the Convent of Los P.P. Dominicos, with a large lectern in the middle.

Capital and lintel adorned with animals in the upper gallery of the Convent of Santa María de las Dueñas.

features a fine wooden roof, supported by torus-shaped arches resting on corbels decorated with leaves and pomegranates.

The Casa de Estudiantes, reached by a tiny door in the De profundis cloister, contains a 17th-century polychrome wood carving of the Virgin, and a Renaissance oratory commissioned by Sotomayor in 1619. The porch is the work of Juan de Ribera (1590-1599) and is situated on the right of the gatehouse, perpendicular to it. It consists of a Tuscan arcaded gallery over which is the library, built in 1683 by José de Churriguera.

Finally, the Claustro de los Aljibes, which communicates with the De profundis cloister, combines artistic elements of various styles. On one side are some splendid Romanesque columns crowned with Isabelline capitals, with semi-circular arches.

San Esteban: interior of the courtyard, affording a glimpse of the delicate forms of the upper gallery and the play of volumes of the church dome.

Convent of Santa María de las Dueñas: one of the loveliest cloisters in Salamanca with, in the background, the cathedrals.

Convent of Santa María de las Dueñas: detail of the floor of the lower gallery, adorned with animal bones.

Convent of Santa María de las Dueñas: a fine panoramic view of the upper gallery.

Convent of Santa María de las Dueñas: the lower gallery of the unique courtyard.

Convent of Santa María de las Dueñas
(Plaza de las Dueñas)

This was founded in 1419 by Juana Rodríguez Maldonado, widow of Juan Sánchez de Sevilla, for noble women. Of the original building remains a tiled Moorish arch, to be seen in the upper gallery of the cloister. The church was rebuilt in Plateresque style in 1522, with a Gothic nave and a front facing east.

The most important feature of the site is the cloister, a veritable jewel of Renaissance art in Salamanca and Spain. It consists of two galleries. The lower gallery has arches crowned by carved capitals with various themes, whilst the upper gallery features some lovely lintels supporting the arches. The authors of the decoration are very likely to have been the same as those responsible for the Palace of Monterrey.

Convent of Nuestra Señora de la Anunciación
(Calle de las Ursulas)

Popularly known as Santa Ursula or Las Ursulas, this convent was founded in 1512 by the patriarch of Alexandria, Alonso de Fonseca. It has a fine Gothic church with a single nave covered by three stellar ribbed vaults In the centre is the tomb of the founder, attributed to Diego de Siloé. On the wall of the Gospel is a niche containing the tomb of the Churchwarden Francisco de Rivas. There are two choirs, the upper choir with a Gothic grille and the lower choir with double coffering of Italian and Mudéjar influence, respectively. The exterior features a polygonal apse reinforced by buttresses with Gothic pinnacles arranged around the 18th-century roof. Between the pilasters is Gothic crenellation.

Convent of
Nuestra
Señora de la
Anunciación,
with the
monument
to
Unamuno.

Altar of the Church of Las Agustinas, now the Church of La Purísima.

The Immaculate Conception, a painting by José de Ribera kept in the Church of La Purísima.

Inside the convent, there is a small museum containing works by Gregorio Fernández, Morales and John of Burgundy.

Convent of Nuestra Señora de la Concepción
(Calle de la Compañía, Calle de Bordadores)

Founded in 1594 by Manuel Fonseca y Zúñiga for a company of Recollet Augustine nuns, this convent is known popularly as the Church of La Purísima. There is confusion regarding the dates of the commencement and completion of the work, but it would seem that the first stone was laid in 1636, the nuns took up

residence in 1641 and the site was finished in 1657. However, the dome collapsed, and in 1676 the cathedral treasurer, Bernardo Ordóñez de Lara, ordered reconstruction work, and the consecration took place in 1687.

The church is in the form of a Latin cross, with large chapels on either side. The pillars are in pairs, and are fluted, whilst the vaults are in the form of lunettes with segmental-arched windows. At the foot of the church is a narrow gallery, and over the crossing rises the dome on the tambour, with lantern and windows. The most impressive feature is the altarpiece of two rows of Corinthian columns with inlaid basement

Convent of Santa Clara: interior with at the rear the lovely Churrigueresque altarpiece.

framing the picture of «La Inmaculada», by Ribera, a work very similar to the painting which must have existed in the Convent of Santa Isabel in Madrid. It is crowned by a crucifix and the statues of Mary Magdalene and the Saints John, in Italian marble. The tabernacle is in lapislazuli, malachite, jasper and gilded bronze, and features statuettes also in gilded bronze. The side altarpieces, on either side of the high chapel, are in the same style. The church also contains several paintings by Ribera: in the nave, «San Jenaro» and the Adoration of the Shepherds. Also interesting are the statues of the Count and Countess of Monterrey, on either side of the high altar, sculpted in Carrara marble.

The front is decorated with fluted Corinthian pilasters on pedestals and entablature, with a fronton with attic in the centre. In the middle is a door with inlaid marble, and at either side are large arches forming a porch with two wings at the corners.

Choir of the Convent of Santa Clara: Centuries-old paintings were discovered on the walls during the 1970s, and their restoration was complete by 1989.

Convent of Santa Clara: interior of the choir.

Convent of Santa Clara
(Calle del Lucero)

The convent was founded in 1220 by Doña Urraca, who wished to live in a hermitage with her female companions. Later, they adopted the rules of Saint Clare. The church has suffered reconstruction various times, and the present Churrigueresque fabric dates back to the 18th century. The altarpiece is also Churrigueresque in inspiration. All that remains from earlier periods is one wing of the cloister, with a roof adorned with Moorish and Gothic elements. The Toledan ceramic altars in the cloister and choir are interesting elements.

Convent of Santa Isabel
(Calle de las Isabeles)

Founded around 1440 by Inés Suárez de Solís for Tertiary Franciscan nuns. The church has a simple 16th-century nave, at whose feet is a choir with beautiful Talaveran tiles. There is a splendid ceiling of Moorish bows and Gothic foliage. The most interesting element is the *al tempera* panel representing Saint Elizabeth of Hungary, by Nicolás Florentino, in the Baroque high altar. In the main chapel are six tombs containing members of the Solís family, dating back to the late 15th and early 16th centuries.

Under the gaze of Friar Luis de León, the Patio de Escuelas, with the front of the University and the former Hospital del Estudio.

UNIVERSITIES AND COLLEGES

Civil University
(Patio de Escuelas)

This is one of the most important buildings in Salamanca, and a jewel of Spanish Renaissance art. The university was founded by Alfonso IX of León when, in 1218, he converted those schools of Salamanca important specialists in the Scriptures into universities. The university was consolidated by Ferdinand III, the Saint, and Alfonso X, the Wise, regulated and extended it in 1254 with the approval of Pope Alexander IV, who conceded Salamanca University the title of General Study, elevating it to the level of Oxford,

Paris or Bologna. The impulse given by Benedict XIII resulted later in the idea of building sites for science classes, and so, from 1415-1433, classrooms were constructed around a rectangular courtyard. The Catholic Monarchs granted the University new privileges, and indeed the façade appears to be a homage to Ferdinand and Isabel. By 1596, Salamanca boasted seventy chairs, including those of: law, theology, medicine, logic and philosophy, rhetoric, grammar, Greek, Latin, Hebrew and Chaldean, astrology and music. Among the illustrious teachers and students here over the history of the university, we can mention Nebrija, Arias Montano, Anaya, Carranza, Malón de Chaide, John of the Cross, Ignatius of Loyola, Beatriz Galindo, Góngora, Friar Luis of León, the

Count-Duke of Olivares, Madina, Soto, Cano, Báñez, Saavedra Fajardo and Unamuno.

The building consists of a chapel dedicated to Saint Jerome, originally located in what is now the vestibule, which has an elegant Moorish ceiling. There now only remain fragments of the old altarpiece by John of Flanders, replaced in the times of Charles III by a marble altarpiece containing the tabernacle by Manuel García Crespo, which was lost in 1812, with six canvases painted by Antonio González Velázquez and Francisco Caciániga. The vault, of which only one third survives, was painted by Fernando Gallego.

The original library, on which construction began in 1472, is now the chapel (described above) as in 1508 it was decided to build the new library, which consists of a large room, bevelled at either end, with a plaster vault by Manuel de Lara y Churriguera. The shelves were added from 1749-1752. There is a Gothic door under a basket-handle arch leading into this repository of over 40,000 volumes including valuable

Door and staircase of the Old Library.

Solemnity and beauty in the Paraninfo of the Civil University.

The Friar Luis de León room in the Civil University. «As we were saying yesterday ...» ▷

incunables and manuscripts. The corridor leading to the library consists of Gothic arches of varying line and a roof of bevelled and Mozarab coffers by Juan de Lara. The staircase begins here, ascending to the upper gallery of the cloister, with a rich bannister adorned with foliage, scrolls and human figures, as well as a Gothic frieze.

Other important rooms, outstanding because of the personages associated with them, include the *paraninfo*, the music room of the Maestro Salinas, the theology faculty and the Fray Luis de León room, with its original structure and the vault in whose keystone bears the coat of arms of the University.

Finally, the most outstanding feature of the University is its façade, a Plateresque masterpiece built from the golden stone of Villamayor. It forms a salient at the entrance to the building and adjoins the library. It was built between 1513 and 1525 - later than the library. It was certainly finished by 1529, as records left by John of Alava prove. The façade consists of three sections: in the centre of the first is a medallion of the Catholic Monarchs; the second contains the coats of arms of the House of Austria, surrounded by busts, medals and an entablature featuring children in amusing postures; and the third has a relief with the coat of arms of the University, flanked by statues, busts and grotesque figures. The author of this artistic jewel is unknown, though it is impossible not to recognise the mark of great artists such as Maestro Egidio of the Cathedral and John of Troy.

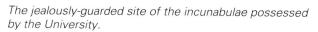
Close-up of the University Chapel.

Physics faculty: detail of the courtyard, with Foucault's pendulum in the centre. ⟩

The jealously-guarded site of the incunabulae possessed by the University.

Peacefulness and purity of line in the Cloister of Las Escuelas Menores.

Escuelas Menores
(Patio de Escuelas)

These were completed in 1533 around one of the most beautiful of all the courtyards of Salamanca, of one body flanked by a gallery of arches supported by thick columns, in which the old classrooms of such subjects as natural history are situated. Some of the paintings by Fernando Gregorio for the ceiling of the original library can still be admired in some of these rooms.

The front is Plateresque and contains two arches featuring the coats of arms of the Emperor and the University. This building is now the seat of the University Museum, entered by a Gothic porch and covered by a fine polychrome coffered ceiling.

Hospital del Estudio
(Patio de Escuelas)

This is now the University rectory but was originally a hospital, said to have been founded before 1469 by Bishop Lope de Barrientos and rebuilt in around 1472. It has a fine front composed of two flat arches within a semicircular arch, with carvings of the Encarnation, Saint Thomas Aquinus and coats of arms. Sculpted foliage and pinnacles crown the building.

College of Archbishop Fonseca, or of Irish Nobles: front and chapel dome.

Colegio Fonseca, or Irish College
(Calle de Fomento)

This college was founded in 1521 by Alonso de Fonseca and was designed to be his last resting-place on his death. Philip II installed here the college for Irish nobles, who came here to escape the persecution to which Catholics were subjected in their country.
The college was built in two stages. The first section, consisting of the rooms, front and the nave of the chapel, was carried out by a master in the style of

Dusk over the lovely courtyard of the College of Archbishop Fonseca, where bullfights were once held.

College of Archbishop Fonseca: courtyard and staircase to the upper gallery.

Palacio de Anaya, in the square of the same name. ▷

John of Alava, except for the porch which is known to have been built by Alonso de Covarrubias. The second stage involved the construction of the chapel sanctuary, the courtyard and the front, by an artist and disciple of Rodrígo Gil. The front is Plateresque and consists of two Ionic sections adorned in the spaces between the columns with medallions and statues, with windows decorated in the same style.

Outstanding inside the church is the transept, higher than the nave, with windows and medallions featuring busts of the Evangelists and university doctors, and the high chapel, with an altarpiece by Berruguete. Both elements have arches and ribbing reminiscent of Gothic architecture.

The courtyard of the college is one of the finest in Salamanca and is a jewel of Spanish Renaissance art. It was designed by Diego de Siloé and constructed, in part, by Pedro de Ibarra. It consists of two galleries of basket-handle arches resting on pies derechos and crowned by a cornice with pinnacles. There are very fine balustrades with four faces and medallions with male and female effigies in the arches.

College of San Bartolomé or of Anaya
(Plaza de Anaya)

Founded in 1401 by Diego de Anaya, archbishop of Seville as the Convent of San Bartolomé, this building was reconstructed in 1760 by Sagarvinaga y Hermosilla and is now the seat of the Faculty of Arts and

The imperial staircase of the Palacio de Anaya, presided over by the peaceful shadow of Miguel de Unamuno.

Calle Campañía, lined by fine buildings. On the left, the Church of El Espíritu Santo, or of Clerecía, and on the right the emblematic Casa de las Conchas.

Sciences. The Chapel of San Esteban has the form of a Latin cross, with Churrigueresque dome and porches.

The hospice is formed by yet another fine Salamancan courtyards, designed by Joaquín de Churriguera and composed of architraved arches where the staircase, presided over by a bust of the former rector, Miguel de Unamuno, begins.

Jesuit College
(Calle de la Compañía)

Also known as the Real Colegio del Espíritu Santo, this is now the seat of the Pontifical University. It was founded in 1611 by Philip III and Margaret of Austria, and designed by the royal architect, Juan Gómez de Mora. The first stone was laid in 1617 and the college

Courtyard of the Pontifical University, with behind it the Church of El Espíritu Santo, or of Clerecía, a magnificent construction sponsored by Margaret of Austria.

Pontifical University: the stairs to the upper storeys, in which some cases are supported by others. The walls bear the names of the erudite scholars who have passed through these rooms.

Filigreed stone crowning the Plateresque front of the University.

Artistic coats of arms carved into the stone of the University front.

dedicated to the Holy Spirit, and it began to be inhabited in 1665, though it was still far from finished. The church, known as the Church of the Clerecía, is in the typically Jesuit style originated by Vignola in the Church of Gesú in Rome. It is decorated with fluted columns and rosettes in the metopes of the frieze. The side chapels have groined vaults and are presided over by Baroque altarpieces, with the statues of the founders in the crossing. On the death of Gómez de Mora, he was succeeded by a Baroque master, who covered the nave with lunette vaults and constructed the dome on an octagonal tambour with a lantern. The high chapel has a typically Salamancan Baroque altarpiece with wreathed columns, by Cristóbal de Honorato, in the centre of which is a relief of the Apparition of the Holy Spirit, over which is repre-

sented the Apparition of the Virgin to Saint Ignatius as he wrote the Spiritual Exercises, and the statues of Saint Augustine, Saint Jerome, Saint Gregory and Saint Basil, crowned by those of the Four Evangelists. The sacristy contains an interesting collection of works, such as «Christ Flagellated», by Carmona, the canvases representing the life of Saint Ignatius, paintings of «Melquisedec» and «The Queen of Sheba», from the studio of Rubens, and the Italian panel of Mary Magdalene.

The front contains elements of various orders, with two rows of Corinthian columns on which rise the towers and the frontispiece, by Andrés García de Quiñones. Six steps lead into the building.

The courtyard, built around enormous Corinthian columns, is one of the finest of Salamancan Baroque

Pontifical University: the beautiful theatre which combines all the plastic arts (p. 68-69).

The coat of arms of the Pontifical University of Salamanca.

patios. It consists of three sections: the lower storey, with round arches, from whose pillars rise the Corinthian columns forming the second section, among which are the balconies, adorned with coats of arms and carved lunettes, and, finally, the third part, whose base is formed by a cornice and which is crowned by a row of pinnacles which, in turn, rest on another cornice. The staircase begins on one side of this courtyard. It is composed of nine flights supported by vaults formed by depressed arches. There is a Baroque meeting room and, after the expulsion of the Jesuits in 1767, was the seat of the Royal Chapel of San Marcos. In 1854 it was converted into a seminario menor, and since 1940 it has been the seat of the Pontifical University.

Plaza de las Agustinas, with the Palace of Monterrey.

Front of the Casa de las Muertes.

PALACES AND HOUSES

Palace of Monterrey
(Plaza de Monterrey)

This palace was constructed by Alonso de Acevedo y Zúñiga, third count of Monterrey and viceroy of Naples, in 1539, according to the plans of Rodrígo Gil de Hontañón, assisted by Martín de Santiago, Pedro de Ibarra and the Aguirres. It is now property of the Duke of Alba.

The palace was planned as a huge rectangle, but only one wing was built, with turrets at the corners. It consists of three sections, the windows adorned with Corinthian columns, frontispieces and the coats of arms of the Fonseca, Zúñiga, Sotomayor, Acevedo, etc, families. The third section features the so-called *paseador de las damas* (Ladies' Walk). The turrets at either corner are a storey higher and are composed of basket-handle arches supporting a broad entablature crowned by Plateresque battlements with pinnacles and chimneys.

Casa de las Muertes
(Calle de Bordadores)

This is a small building with a magnificent Plateresque façade decorated with grotesques, mouldings and busts. The doorway is outstanding, with a lintel framed by the mouldings which run around the entire building, resembling a frieze full of grotesques, with a coat of arms surrounded by a laurel wreath sustained by two Cupids. Over the door, the main balcony is adorned with pillasters and the coat of arms and bust of Fonseca. On either side are lovely windows sculpted in the same style, whilst the façade is crowned by a carved cornice featuring floral decoration and cherubins.

The «House of the Dead» is so called due to the legendary events which are said to have occurred in it. In 1898, the historian Bolanegra recorded a version which claimed that the Monroys and the Manzanos, rival families during the 15th century, came to blows, and that two deaths ensued. Years later, when the house was built, the bodies of these unfortunates were found, along with two headless cadavers, said to be the brothers decapitated by María la Brava. Another legend holds that in the cellar of the house was a murderer, who killed the members of a priest's family. However, the most plausible version is that the house takes its name from the skulls carved in the windows, a common element in Plateresque decoration, or from the name of the street where it stands, which dates back to 1753. The house was the residence of the Ibarra family until 1805, when it was

Detail of the artistic decoration in the elegant courtyard of the Palacio de Fonseca.

Front of the Palacio de Fonseca, now the seat of the provincial government.

auctioned publicly in accordance with a decree dated 19 September 1789. Next to it is the house of Unamuno, with the coat of arms of the Ovalles.

Casa de los Fonseca
(Calle de San Pablo)

Also known as the House of Salt, as it was used as a salt store, this building is now the seat of the Provincial Deputation. It was built by Alfonso de Fonseca in 1538, and features a fine front, with three storeys. The first is composed of four arches resting on columns and adorned with medallions. The second storey has three balconies flanked by columns and carved grotesques, and the third features eight arches and is adorned by the Fonseca arms and carved cherubins.

The interior of the building contains a splendid Renaissance courtyard, of irregular shape. It is entered under an arch resting on four flying corbels. At the top is a gallery supported by flying mensules, whose carved figures are reputed to have been intended to ridicule some Salamancan noblemen, relatives of Fonseca, who behaved unchivalrously towards María de Ulloa. The left wall has a portico of seven semi-circular arches, whilst the front is reminiscent of the Casa de las Conchas.

In the same street are the Palace of Solís and the House of Diego Maldonado, servant of Fonseca.

House of Doña María la Brava
(Plaza de los Bandos)

A 15th-century building which belonged to María la Brava. It features a fine balcony crowned by a frieze of grotesques, with the coat of arms of the Enríquez family.

The house is in harmony with the Palace of

One of the most historic squares in the city: Plaza de los Bandos, with in the foreground (right) the House of María la Brava.

Palacio de Figueroa, now the city casino.

House of Saint Theresa.

Torre del Clavero. ▷

Garcigrande, situated in the same square, with a lovely Plateresque front adorned with the coats of arms of the Espinosa, Guzmán, Girón and Maldonado lineages.

House of Santa Teresa
(Plaza de Santa Teresa)

Also known as the House of Los Ovalle, this was constructed at the same time as that of María la Brava. It was here that Saint Theresa of Avila spent her first night in Salamanca, in 1570.

The slender silhouette of the Torre del Aire.

College of Calatrava
(Calle de Francisco Montejo)

This is now the Diocesan Seminary, and was built by Joaquín de Churriguera in 1717, the characteristic style receiving certain modifications at the hands of Jovellanos at the end of the 18th century. The building formerly belonged to the Order of Calatrava.

OTHER INTERESTING BUILDINGS

Torre del Clavero
(Calle del Consuelo/Calle de Miñagustín)

According to tradition, this tower forms the remains of the mansion of Francisco de Sotomayor, keeper of the keys of the Order of Alcántara in 1470, though it is also said to have belonged to Friar Diego de Anaya. The building has the appearance of a fortress, with turrets in the bevelled sections and a cornice of arches and modillions featuring the coats of arms of the Sotomayor and Anaya families.

Torre del Aire
(Calle del Aire)

This forms part of the Palace of Fermoselle, and is built in Italianate style, with arched windows and Gothic carvings.

Casa de las Conchas
(Calle de las Compañías)

The «House of Shells» was built at the start of the 16th century by Rodrígo Arias de Maldonado, Knight of the Order of Santiago. This is one of the best-known buildings in Salamanca, distinguished by the shells adorning its front. The history of the house is uncertain, but it would appear that, as Rodrígo was a Knight of Santiago, it would be logical to employ the most common symbol of the Order. The Maldonado coat of arms (five fleurs-de-lis) also appears on the walls and around the windows, supported variously by angels, sirens or lions, or wreathed in laurel. This coat of arms, together with the shells, symbol of the Pimentels, formed a prelude to the wedding of Juana Pimentel and Rodrígo Maldonado.

The front features three different Gothic grilles, whilst the decoration is unmistakably Italian, though the actual author is not known. The front contains the coat of arms of the Catholic Monarch.

The interior has a fine courtyard, with two storeys. The lower section is formed by arches of various types supported by square pillars, whilst the segmental arches of the upper storey rest on columns made from Carrara marble, surrounded by a splendid crenallated handrail. The parapets bear the coat of

Close-up of the Maldonado coat of arms on the front of the Casa de las Conchas.

arms of the Maldonados, and gargoyles. The balustrade is adorned with lions and coats of arms, whilst the ceiling features large square and hexagonal coffers.

Roman bridge

Thought to have been constructed during the reign of Trajan, forming part of the Roman road known as the Vía de la Plata from Astorga to Mérida, passing through Salamanca. The bridge is formed by fifteen arches, some of which have been restored. Entering the city over this bridge, one finds an interesting Iberian bull, mentioned in the novel «Lazarillo de Tormes».

The Roman bridge commands views of the Tormes, described by such writers as Friary Luis de León. From the river, there are fine views of the cathedral towers and those of La Clerecía and the Convent of San Esteban, as well as an overall view of the city, whose white and golden stone from Villamayor takes on extraordinary tones at dusk.

Horizontal and vertical lines, the cathedrals and the Roman bridge, a truly enchanting sight.

SQUARES, GARDENS AND STREETS

Plaza Mayor and the City Hall

Plaza Mayor is one of the most beautiful squares in Spain, matched only by the Plaza Mayor in Madrid. It was built from 1729 according to plans drawn up by Alberto de Churriguera. The east side was completed in 1733, and the north side and the City Hall were finished in 1755. On the death of Alberto de Churriguera, Andrés García de Quinoñes took over

the direction of the work, along with the sculptor José de Lara y Churriguera, who carved the medallions in the spandrels of the arches, with monarchs and illustrious personages. The City Hall boasts a series of elements dating back to 1852. The east front contains the Royal Pavilion, over the arch of Calle de Toro, from where the Spanish monarchs watched the bullfights. The north side contains the City Hall, which consists of a splendid Baroque palace of two storeys, with Corinthian columns, between which are balconies crowned by frontons. The sections are separated by

projecting cornices, whilst at the top there is a frieze imitating Greek triglyphs and metopes. The belltower is outstanding, consisting of three semicircular arches flanked by Ionic columns. Each arch houses one of the three bells.

Campo de San Francisco
(Calle de Ramón y Cajal)

This is one of the city's most privileged viewpoints, commanding a panoramic view of Salamanca. It is situated in one of finest areas of this lovely city, reached via Plaza de la Fuente and Calle de las Sorias. It is found behind the Palace of Monterrey, beside the Rincón de las Ursulas and the Church of the Vera Cruz, close to the house of Unamuno, the House of Las Muertes, the Church of Santa María de los Caballeros and that of the Recollet Augustines. Not in vain did Unamuno, former rector of the university, immortalise this splendid corner in admirable verse.

The streets of Salamanca

The centre of the city is, without doubt, the Plaza Mayor, a squares which, with Plaza Mayor, Madrid, and Plaza del Obradoiro, Santiago, approaches perfection in terms of balance and attractiveness. This central square can form the starting-point for the most varied strolls through the streets which have their origin here, for, as we have said before, Salamanca is a veritable architectural museum.
Beginning at the Church of San Martín, its back to the square, take Rúa Mayor towards the cathedrals.

Salamanca City Hall: Reception Room.

The steps of the City Hall: a detail of the railings. ▷

Along this street, we can admire the Casa de las Conchas and the front of the Clerecía. This main thoroughfare ends in Plaza de Anaya, containing the Colegio de San Bartolomé and the New Cathedral. The tiny streets around the cathedrals have a flavour and an atmosphere all their own, Calle de Tentenecio, for instance, which winds down to the Tenerías district and the Tormes, where we can contemplate the Roman bridge, the «Iberian Bull» and the Church of Santiago. From here, go back up to the area around the cathedrals, taking Calle de Libreros, where we encounter Plaza Fray Luis de León, one of the most

Sessions Chamber of Salamanca City Hall.

Calle Toro.

Campo de San Francisco. ▷

important squares, featuring the front of the University, the Patio de Escuelas, the City Museum and the Hospital de Estudio.

Continuing along Calle de Libreros, we come to the Clerecía, where we take Calle de la Compañía, visiting the Pontifical University, the palaces of Maldonado and Solís, the magnificent surrounds of the Church of San Benito. At the end of these grand slopes is a fine view of the Convent of Agustinas Recoletas and the Church of La Purísima, and the charming Plaza de Monterrey, containing the palace of the same name. At the rear of this square, take Calle Ramón y Cajal to the Colegio de los Irlandeses (on the left) and the Campo de San Francisco (on the right). Going around

these gardens, we come to the Rincón de las Ursulas, featuring the statue of Fonseca, and Calle de Bordadores, with the House of Las Muertes and that of Unamuno. Further along the same street is Plaza de Santa Teresa and, on the right, Plaza de los Bandos, flanked by magnificent palaces and mansions such as those of María la Brava and Garcigrande. Nearby is Plaza de San Boal. Calle Zamora starts out from Plaza de los Bandos, leading us back once more to Plaza Mayor.

If we take any of the little streets branching out from Plaza Mayor, we can walk around Plaza del Mercado, contemplating such interesting sites as Plaza de Sexmeros and the modern Gran Vía. Take Calle de

SᴬⁿFRANCISCO DE ASIS

LOADO SEAS MI SEÑOR
POR TODAS LAS CRIATURAS

Alamedilla Park.

San Pablo, leading to Plaza de Colón, admiring the Torre del Clavero and, finally, reaching Plaza de Santo Domingo to visit the convents of Las Dueñas and San Esteban.

The historic centre of Salamanca is enclosed within the avenues of Canalejas, San Vicente, Carmelitas and Mirat, all of which conserve the original golden coloured stone. Beyond the ring-road, the city expanded long ago, and a new Salamanca was built, with industrial estates and residential zones. Modern architectural styles are amply demonstrated in roads such as Federico Anaya, Portugal, Torres Villarroel and Avenida de Italia.

MUSEUMS

Unamuno House-Museum
(Calle de Libreros)

The museum displays objects and documents written by the famous former rector of Salamanca University, Miguel de Unamuno y Jugo, and is contained in the house where Unamuno lived for several years. Work began on the museum in 1952 and it was opened to the public the following year. In 1968, the Ministry of Education and Science acquired the collections from the heirs, and they now pertain to the University. The House-Museum was reorganised in 1977, with the creation of a centre of reference and bibliography on the life and work of Unamuno, open to researchers.

One side of Plaza de los Bandos.

Diocesan Museum
(Old Cathedral, Plaza de Anaya)

This was created by the Cathedral Council on 15 November 1950 with objects from the cathedrals and other churches in the diocese. The museum was officially opened on 15 March 1953, and its collections are housed in the chapterhouse and adjoining dependencies. Outstanding are: the rooms dedicated to the work of Fernando Gallego, a Salamancan painter, and his school; the «Triptych» by John of Flanders; and the cases containing an «Abrideira» Virgin in ivory, a number of Limoges enamels and fragments of Moorish art and the silverwork in the sacristy.

City Museum
(Former Episcopal Palace, Plaza de Juan XXIII)

This was created on 31 October 1979 by the Cultural Committee of the City Council, and contains objects and documents concerning the history of the city,

Alto soto de torre ... a view from the incomparable Huerto de Calixto y Melibea.

An overall view of the Parque Fluvial, on the banks of the River Tormes.

The House of Unamuno.

formerly scattered amongst various Council dependencies. It was opened on 13 January 1980 in the Torre del Clavero, but in 1986 was transferred to its present site, a building the diocese has granted to the City Council for a period of 30 years.

Salamanca Museum
(Plaza del Patio de Escuelas)

A museum created on 25 May 1846 with objects collected by the Provincial Commission for Monuments, housed in the library of San Bartolomé. It was opened on 1 October 1848 in the College of San Bartolomé, and in 1864 was transferred to the Convent of San Esteban, where it remained until 1936. It was then moved to the Escuelas Menores and, in 1949, to the Palace of Abarca Maldonado in the Patio de Escuelas, purchased for the purpose by the Ministry of Education and Science. The palace was reor-

The «Triptych of Saint Catherine,» by Fernando Gallego.

ganised between 1970 and 1974, and meanwhile the collections were displayed in the Casa de las Conchas. The museum has also been known by three different names: the Provincial Fine Arts Museum, the Fine Arts Museum of Salamanca and, finally, the Salamanca Museum. It has three sections, on archaeology, fine arts and popular art.

The Palace of Albarca is a 15th-century building which formerly belonged to Alvarez Abarca, Isabel the Catholic's doctor. The museum contains collections of 16th- and 17th-century sculpture, painting from the 15th to the 20th centuries and decorative arts, such as furniture and silverwork, as well as interesting archaeological objects and elements from buildings long since lost.

POPULAR CUSTOMS, CRAFTS AND GASTRONOMY

Popular customs

The folklore of Salamanca revolves around Holy Week, with the traditional processions of the *cofradías* (brotherhoods) and the heightened solemnity of the services held at the chapel of the university over this period.

Also important are the festivities of San John of Sahagún on 12 June and of the Virgin of the Vega, patron saint of Salamanca, on 8 September.

The local celebrations includes corridas and dances (known here as *charradas*) performed to the sound of

For a few hours during the 5th Centenary, Plaza Mayor was converted into a bullring, and a corrida staged.

the dulcimer and the drum. Popular are the *jota castellana*, the *baile de la rosca* and, particularly, the *baile del asentao,* a dance of little movement from the waist up, but of frenetic activity in the feet. Many of these dances are accompanied by popular songs, such as *tonadas, rondas,* marriage songs and «songs of passion».

Most of these folklore and cultural events are staged in Plaza Mayor or in the university grounds. There are also musical seasons, conferences, exhibitions, as well as congresses which choose this historic city. Commemorations have been held here celebrating the Castilian tongue, or figures like Saint Theresa, Friar Luis of León, Miguel de Unamuno (on the fiftieth anniversary of his death) and many more, bringing together important personages, with exhibitions of important artistic, bibliographic and documentary collections. Summer courses are also organised for Spanish and foreign students alike, attracting young people from universities all over the world here to study Spanish or other subjects.

Salamanca is historically linked with the bull, and its inhabitants feel closely identified with any event connected with this noble animal, symbol of the city. Cattle fairs are held just outside and in the surrounding towns, whilst *corridas* take place during the annual festivities, revealing the passion felt by many locals for such a sport.

But we must speak of the *charro*, or traditional dress of Salamanca, one of the richest national costumes in

Watchful bulls, with the ancient oak trees of Campo Charro.

Spain. That of the man consists of plain corduroy trousers, worn tight at the leg, with buttoned gaiters. A black sash is worn around the waist, under a short jacket revealing the waistcoat. On holidays, these articles are adorned with richly-coloured embroidery and silver buttons, replacing the metallic buttons for everyday use. The woman wears a mantle, a velvet shawl and blouse with colourful frills, the entire costume decked with sequins, gold and gilded fringes. The short sleeves are in a matching style, whilst the hair is parted down the middle, with three large plaited buns, to which a lace headscarf is attached by silver pins. The costume is complete by rich golden earrings, rings, necklaces and brooches. Though this charro dress is the most elaborate and splendid in the province, there are also many varieties worth mentioning, such as the dresses of Armuña, or of the plains, as well as those of the mountains of Peña de Francia, La Alberca, Gredos or Candelario, La Ribera and El Rebollar.

Crafts

Salamancan crafts centre on filigrana charra, made particularly around Ciudad-Rodrigo and the Portuguese frontier, available in the jewellers' and gift shops of the city. This is fine gold or silver work, originally made to adorn the *charro* dress, but whose range has now extended enormously to include, besides buttons, earrings, rings, bracelets and hair-

Pottery in one of the puestos held at different times of the year.

pins for the regional costumes, keyrings, cufflinks, brooches and tieclips, not to mention an infinite variety of designs in earrings, chains, rings, and so on, created by a school of designers around the famous charra artistry.

Other important craft industries are leather, with the manufacture of riding boots and other accessories for this sport; cowbells; embroidery, such as that of the mountain region of La Aberca; and pottery, metalwork, wickerwork, etc, principally for agricultural purposes.

Gastronomy

The cuisine of Salamanca is based, essentially, on meat dishes. Cattle and game, with pulses, are the staple elements of the local diet, with specialities in sausagemeat products, ham, pork and *chorizo*, particularly that from Guijuelo and El Payo. Chanfaina is a rich dish made with rice, game and lamb, with pieces of chorizo. *Farinato* is made with lard, bread and paprika, eaten with fried eggs, and is a typical dish in Ciudad-Rodrigo. *Hornazo* is made with local sausage meats. *Calderillo* is a lamb dish with a rich sauce, whilst roast lamb and suckling pig are popular here, along with stewed tongue, fried pork pieces, Castilian garlic soup (here garnished with the famous Iberian ham), game dishes using pieces from the nearby fields and woodlands - deer, boar, partridge, pheasant etc, and fish from the trout-rich rivers of the frontier and the sierra.

Local wines include reds from the Sierra de Francia and the clarets of the Ribera del Duero. Many of the finest wines sampled in Salamanca are from Zamora and Valladolid.

Turning to desserts, we must acclaim the cheeses from Hinojosa del Duero, as well as sweets and cakes such as the *maimon*, the *chocho* and the *altramuz*, not to mention the almond-based *almendras garrapiñadas de Santa Teresa*, *roscas de Saucelle* and *rosquillas de Ledesma*.

The most typical restaurants are to be found in the historic centre of the city, the University quarter and around the cathedrals, as well as the market district. Popular eating-houses are the *mesones*, where we can take lunch or dinner, or enjoy a midday apéritif or a late nightcap.

CONTENTS

We should like to express our gratitude to the individuals and institutions of Salamanca who gave their assistance to the preparation of this book.

Collection ALL EUROPE

	Spanish	French	English	German	Italian	Catalan	Dutch	Swedish	Portuguese	Japanese	Finnish
1 ANDORRA	•										
2 LISBON	•										
3 LONDON	•										
4 BRUGES	•										
5 PARIS	•										
6 MONACO	•										
7 VIENNA	•										
11 VERDUN	•										
12 THE TOWER OF LONDON	•										
13 ANTWERP	•										
14 WESTMINSTER ABBEY	•										
15 THE SPANISH RIDING SCHOOL IN VIENNA	•										
16 FATIMA	•										
17 WINDSOR CASTLE	•										
19 COTE D'AZUR	•										
22 BRUSSELS	•										
23 SCHÖNBRUNN PALACE	•										
24 ROUTE OF PORT WINE	•										
26 HOFBURG PALACE	•										
27 ALSACE	•										
31 MALTA	•										
32 PERPIGNAN	•										
33 STRASBOURG	•										
34 MADEIRA + PORTO SANTO											
35 CERDAGNE - CAPCIR											
36 BERLIN	•										

Collection ART IN SPAIN

	Spanish	French	English	German	Italian	Catalan	Dutch	Swedish	Portuguese	Japanese	Finnish
1 PALAU DE LA MUSICA CATALANA	•		•		•						
2 GAUDI	•	•	•	•	•					•	
3 PRADO MUSEUM I (Spanish Painting)	•	•	•	•	•					•	
4 PRADO MUSEUM II (Foreign Painting)	•	•	•	•	•						
5 MONASTERY OF GUADALUPE	•										
6 THE CASTLE OF XAVIER	•	•	•								
7 THE FINE ARTS MUSEUM OF SEVILLE	•	•	•	•	•						
8 SPANISH CASTLES	•	•	•	•							
9 THE CATHEDRALS OF SPAIN	•	•	•								
10 THE CATHEDRAL OF GERONA	•	•	•								
14 PICASSO	•	•	•		•					•	
15 REALES ALCAZARES (ROYAL PALACE OF SEVILLE)	•	•	•	•							
16 MADRID'S ROYAL PALACE	•	•	•	•							
17 ROYAL MONASTERY OF EL ESCORIAL	•	•	•	•							
18 THE WINES OF CATALONIA	•	•	•								
19 THE ALHAMBRA AND THE GENERALIFE	•	•	•	•							
20 GRANADA AND THE ALHAMBRA	•										
21 ROYAL ESTATE OF ARANJUEZ	•	•	•	•							
22 ROYAL ESTATE OF EL PARDO	•	•	•	•							
23 ROYAL HOUSES	•	•	•	•							
24 ROYAL PALACE OF SAN ILDEFONSO	•	•	•	•							
25 HOLY CROSS OF THE VALLE DE LOS CAIDOS	•	•	•	•							
26 OUR LADY OF THE PILLAR OF SARAGOSSA	•	•	•								
27 TEMPLE DE LA SAGRADA FAMILIA	•	•	•	•	•	•					
28 POBLET ABTEI	•	•	•		•						

Collection ALL SPAIN

	Spanish	French	English	German	Italian	Catalan	Dutch	Swedish	Portuguese	Japanese	Finnish
1 ALL MADRID	•	•	•	•	•					•	
2 ALL BARCELONA	•	•	•	•	•						
3 ALL SEVILLE	•	•	•	•	•						
4 ALL MAJORCA	•	•	•	•	•						
5 ALL THE COSTA BRAVA	•	•	•	•	•						
6 ALL MALAGA and the Costa del Sol	•	•	•	•	•			•			
7 ALL THE CANARY ISLANDS (Gran Canaria)	•	•	•	•	•			•	•		
8 ALL CORDOBA	•	•	•	•	•					•	
9 ALL GRANADA	•	•	•	•	•					•	
10 ALL VALENCIA	•	•	•	•	•						
11 ALL TOLEDO	•	•	•	•	•						
12 ALL SANTIAGO	•	•	•	•	•						
13 ALL IBIZA and Formentera	•	•	•	•	•						
14 ALL CADIZ and the Costa de la Luz	•	•	•	•	•						
15 ALL MONTSERRAT	•	•	•	•	•						
16 ALL SANTANDER and Cantabria	•	•	•	•	•						
17 ALL THE CANARY ISLANDS II, (Tenerife)	•	•	•	•	•				•	•	•
20 ALL BURGOS	•	•	•	•	•						
21 ALL ALICANTE and the Costa Blanca	•	•	•	•				•			
22 ALL NAVARRA	•	•	•	•							
23 ALL LERIDA	•	•	•	•		•					
24 ALL SEGOVIA	•	•	•	•							
25 ALL SARAGOSSA	•	•	•	•							
26 ALL SALAMANCA	•	•	•	•					•		
27 ALL AVILA	•	•	•	•							
28 ALL MINORCA	•	•	•	•							
29 ALL SAN SEBASTIAN and Guipúzcoa	•										
30 ALL ASTURIAS	•		•								
31 ALL LA CORUNNA and the Rías Altas	•	•	•								
32 ALL TARRAGONA	•	•	•								
33 ALL MURCIA	•	•	•								
34 ALL VALLADOLID	•	•	•								
35 ALL GIRONA	•	•	•								
36 ALL HUESCA	•	•									
37 ALL JAEN	•	•	•								
38 ALL ALMERIA	•	•	•								
40 ALL CUENCA	•	•	•								
41 ALL LEON	•	•	•								
42 ALL PONTEVEDRA, VIGO and the Rías Bajas	•	•	•								
43 ALL RONDA	•	•	•								
44 ALL SORIA	•										
46 ALL EXTREMADURA	•										
47 ALL ANDALUSIA	•	•	•		•						
52 ALL MORELLA	•	•			•						

Collection ALL AMERICA

	Spanish	French	English	German	Italian	Catalan	Dutch	Swedish	Portuguese	Japanese	Finnish
1 PUERTO RICO	•		•								
2 SANTO DOMINGO	•		•								
3 QUEBEC			•	•							
4 COSTA RICA	•		•								
5 CARACAS	•										

Collection ALL AFRICA

	Spanish	French	English	German	Italian	Catalan	Dutch	Swedish	Portuguese	Japanese	Finnish
1 MOROCCO	•	•	•	•	•						
2 THE SOUTH OF MOROCCO	•	•	•	•	•						
3 TUNISIA	•	•	•								
4 RWANDA		•									

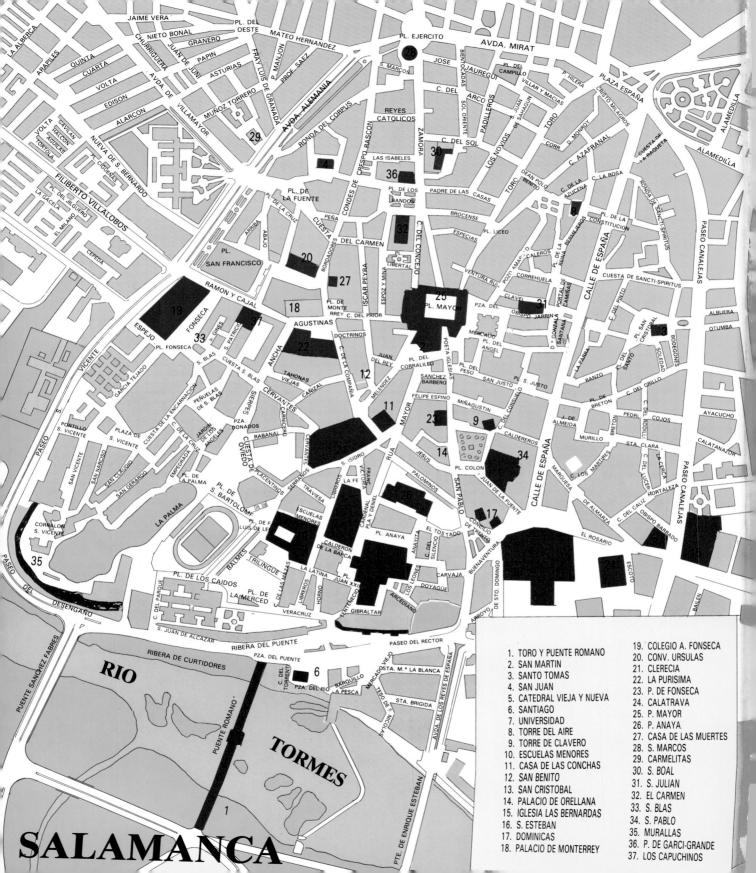

SALAMANCA

RIO TORMES

1. TORO Y PUENTE ROMANO
2. SAN MARTIN
3. SANTO TOMAS
4. SAN JUAN
5. CATEDRAL VIEJA Y NUEVA
6. SANTIAGO
7. UNIVERSIDAD
8. TORRE DEL AIRE
9. TORRE DE CLAVERO
10. ESCUELAS MENORES
11. CASA DE LAS CONCHAS
12. SAN BENITO
13. SAN CRISTOBAL
14. PALACIO DE ORELLANA
15. IGLESIA LAS BERNARDAS
16. S. ESTEBAN
17. DOMINICAS
18. PALACIO DE MONTERREY
19. COLEGIO A. FONSECA
20. CONV. URSULAS
21. CLERECIA
22. LA PURISIMA
23. P. DE FONSECA
24. CALATRAVA
25. P. MAYOR
26. P. ANAYA
27. CASA DE LAS MUERTES
28. S. MARCOS
29. CARMELITAS
30. S. BOAL
31. S. JULIAN
32. EL CARMEN
33. S. BLAS
34. S. PABLO
35. MURALLAS
36. P. DE GARCI-GRANDE
37. LOS CAPUCHINOS